Yes, I do Love you!

A Children's Song and Story by Kaycee Lynne

SECOND EDITION

tate publishing
CHILDREN'S DIVISION

Published by Tate Publishing & Enterprises, LLC
127 E. Trade Center Terrace | Mustang, Oklahoma 73064 USA
1.888.361.9473 | www.tatepublishing.com

Tate Publishing is committed to excellence in the publishing industry. The company reflects the philosophy established by the founders, based on Psalm 68:11,
"The Lord gave the word and great was the company of those who published it."

Book design copyright © 2013 by Tate Publishing, LLC. All rights reserved.

Published in the United States of America

ISBN: 978-1-62563-405-4
1. Family & Relationships / General
2. Pets / General
13.02.06

OPEN YOUR HEART AND BELIEVE THAT LIFE CAN SEND
ENOUGH LOVE TO GO AROUND.

Kaycee Lynne

I love you more than the deep blue sea

More than the sun in the sky

More than the stars and the moon

I love you! Yes I do! Yes I do! Yes I do!

I love you more than the grass that grows

More than the wind that blows

From your head down to your toes

I love you! Yes I do! Yes I do! Yes I do!

Yes, I do love you. Yes I do.

Yes, I do love you. Yes I do.

Yes, I do love you. Yes I do.

Yes I do! Yes I do! Yes I do!

I love you more than a big surprise

More than a favourite ride

More than money can buy

I love you! Yes I do! Yes I do! Yes I do!

I love you more than words can say

More than fun and play

At the end of every day

I love you! Yes I do! Yes I do! Yes I do!

Yes, I do love you. Yes I do.

Yes, I do love you. Yes I do.

Yes, I do love you. Yes I do.

Yes I do! Yes I do! Yes I do!

The End.